Dedicated to my wife Lorraine

About the Author

Born and raised on a small farm in Oregon, I am always been connected to hard work and the great outdoors. After joining the Army and serving for three years, including a memorable year stationed in Korea, I returned to civilian life with a wealth of experiences. From working in sawmills to joining Boeing, I never shied away from new challenges. In 1977, I ventured into the real estate world, followed by a successful career in the loan business, where I remains active to this day.

Despite my professional achievements, writing has always been a source of fun and creativity for me. With no formal training, I began crafting humorous letters for a fishing club I belongs to, and that spark of joy in writing led me to explore the world of fantasy. Armed with a vivid imagination, I decided to try my hand at fantasy writing, combining my whimsical ideas with my passion for storytelling.

Outside of writing, I am also an avid collector. I own a small collection of classic cars, stored in a warehouse filled with an array of neon and porcelain signs and vintage clocks. My love for all things automotive has been a constant source of inspiration and enjoyment.

Table of Contents

The Four Horsemen of the Apocalypse

It was a beautiful, warm spring day, and I had hiked a fair distance up to a creek in a lush meadow on land managed by the U.S. Bureau of Land Management. As an experienced university-trained aquatic biologist, I work for the Department of Forestry in the Stanislaus National Forest. The land was leased out to a large private cattle company, and my department was investigating the effect that cattle manure and urine, logging, off-road vehicles, discharge in culverts, etc., affect aquatic organisms in the creek.

I got startled and looked up as I heard the sound of hooves and saw four horsemen quickly riding toward me. Their large armored steeds came to an abrupt, snorting stop a few feet before running me over.

With false bravado, I asked them who they were. And what were they doing here. In a rough gravelly voice, the first of the four hideous devil riders introduced himself as *The Demon of Famine*. He said, "We are the Four Horseman of the Apocalypse—*Pestilence, War, Famine, and Death. Pestilence* has already spread the deadly Coronavirus your world is suffering from now, and the rest will follow soon. *War* has already commenced in some of your countries. *Famine* and *Death* will soon follow. There is absolutely no hope for humankind in your world. The curses we have unleashed on your people cannot be stopped. Our Master will rule over the Upper World and the Underworld. He has commanded us to come for you."

"Who is your master," I asked. "And why me?"

"We do not question our Master. Your kind calls him by various names—like Dark Lord, Lucifer, Satan, or the Devil, etc. Egyptians call him *Set*, the Hindus *Shiva*, *Tchort* to Russians, and so on. We will take you to Gbezx, who will be your guide. He is waiting close by."

I summoned some more false courage and refused to go.

"You have no choice. You cannot deny us, or we will destroy you. So choose wisely, come with us to meet our Master, or we will have to eliminate you now—right here on the spot."

Obviously, at this point, I didn't have many options. We traveled a couple of miles through the woods and came to a large ancient oak tree. One of the Horseman took his lance, pushed it firmly against the tree, and a well-disguised door opened. *The Demon of War* roughly shoved me forward—just as a strange, frightful creature came through the door.

He was around my height of 5'7" tall and was a garish reddish brown in color. He had a long, curved tail, and his feet had split hooves like a cow. Spiked horns came out of his head. He had a long, sharp, hooked nose, red eyes, and long sharp teeth. His tongue was black. And forked like a serpent. He told me in a surprisingly pleasant voice that he was Gbezx. He authoritatively waved his hand to dismiss the horsemen, who turned and simply disappeared after a short distance—it was almost as if they evaporated.

Gbezx said he had studied my personal and professional profile in detail and that he may have a position for me to assist him in gathering the information he needs from here on Earth. He claimed to be one of the leaders of the Underworld and reports directly to The Master.

He placed his claw-like hand on my arm to guide me to meet The Master. We entered a small, dank elevator where he pushed a single red button, and we descended at a very fast rate of speed for less than a minute. The door opened and deposited us in a huge windowless room with at least 80-foot ceilings. The air was still, humid, and foul-smelling, and the temperature was easily 100 degrees.

I fearfully asked if I was going to have to live down here. He laughed a strangely melodious laugh and said;

"No, you will live in the Upper World and perform the tasks I give you. You will have plenty of money and will be required to travel the world. I know you speak three languages now, and we will teach you a few more, depending on where I send you."

He motioned to a couple of devil-like creatures carrying tridents to approach. They bowed their heads to him as he spoke to them in a strange guttural language. One moved to the front of us, and the other one followed behind.

We walked along a path on the side of the room and came to an area where there were a number of what I assumed were humans working on some kind of machine. I asked Gbezx what they were making. He said it was various items that they needed, but it wasn't necessary that I knew what they were. Some of the winged devils had whips and would strike the workers if they weren't working as hard as the devils apparently thought they should. A winged devil flew over, easily picked up one of the workers, and quickly flew off down the hall. Just as quickly, another devil carried in a replacement worker and set him in front of the machine the other one had vacated.

It was very noisy and smelled horribly foul, like Sulphur or rotten eggs. There was a cacophony of pleading, crying, and moaning, along with bitter cursing and swearing. When I asked him where these people lived and what they ate, he laughed his eerily melodious laugh and said that dead people didn't eat. I told Gbezx I thought when humans died, their bodies stayed on Earth. He said their shell bodies are formed around their souls when they come to Hades. After they have no further use to us, you will see in a while how we dispose of them. Remember, thousands of them come here every day.

When I asked him how old he was, he said;

"I am tens of hundreds of years old. I was here when your false prophet Jesus was alive and when Pontius Pilate came down here. You will see Pilate later, as he is in the Hall of Heroes. "How old is the Dark Lord?" I asked. "He was the being who gave the apple to Eve in the Garden of Eden, so you figure it out," he replied.

Thinking this was just incredible and suspending my disbelief, we continued our walk and came to a huge room. The center of the room contained a large 200-foot diameter cauldron full of molten lava. On the one side was a long, wide ramp leading up to the edge. A constant stream of hundreds of zombie-like people lumbered up the ramp and into the red-hot flaming lava. They were being herded up by the winged devils, and they seemed to vaporize instantly.

Gbezx explained that their souls had been separated from their body shells through a very complicated procedure he wouldn't try to explain to me. I thought they likely gave or sold their soul to the devil. We watched them as we continued down the path. We took a right turn down another path and came to a round room about 40 feet wide with a large table that almost filled the room. Sitting around the table were body shells, but on each was a perfect head of what must be most all of the infamous tyrants who have ever lived. Gbezx named them for me, pointing out, for example, Julius Caesar, Pontius Pilate, Attila the Hun, Genghis Khan, Vladimir Lenin, Joseph Stalin, Adolf Hitler, Benito Mussolini, Mao Zedong, Pol Pot, Idi Amin, Saddam Hussein, Muammar Gaddafi, and some others I didn't recognize.

It was completely chaotic, as they were each speaking simultaneously in their own language—it was loud and, of course, made no sense as they swung their heads back and forth, chattering away. It was pure bedlam, bizarre and unsettling! Gbezx said this scene was one of his Master's hobbies. He would come by periodically, and since he speaks hundreds of languages, he could understand all of them. Even while they just chattered on nonsensically.

Gbezx seemed to realize that I was uncomfortable and would like to leave. He smiled and motioned our guards for us to escort us out. As we continued down the path, it was burning hot on the bottom of my shoes. I was glad I was still wearing my hiking boots with their thick soles.

I queried Gbezx about his life and his diet. He said it is rather complicated but that they absorb the nutrients in the air that are generated from certain rocks that line the walls and ceilings. He solicitously inquired if I was hungry and took me to a room that had cupboards containing round items that were about the same shape as an English muffin. He said there were various flavors to choose from, and they were very tasty and nutritious.

Gbezx said I was not to speak to the five other beings in the room. They were sitting at small separate tables and were eating disks and drinking a clear liquid. There appeared to be two Asians, a Black, and two Whites. First I tried the muffins/disks. It had a pleasant lemon flavor. I told Gbezx I needed to find a toilet. He said we would soon be in an area that had hot volcanic stones where I could relieve myself on one of the stones, and my waste would be vaporized instantly.

He told me the cavern we were in extended for hundreds of miles. We continued to walk down the path. Where it split off, we went to the right and came to a room that had a devil seated at a reception desk. After Gbezx and the devil spoke, he turned to me and announced we would soon go in to meet The Master.

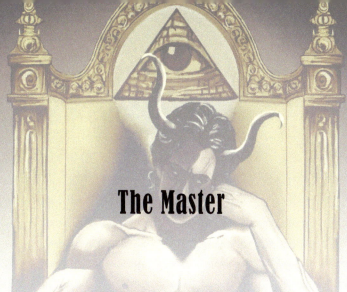

The Master

The door to the room was opened by a devil guard, but the receptionist went in and came back out in a few minutes and motioned for us to enter. The room was about 50 feet square with 30-foot ceilings. I was a bit awe-struck as The Master/Lucifer was sitting on a massive golden throne. He was huge. I would guess eight feet tall and with a chiseled, muscular body that was reddish in color like Gbezx. He had large horns that appeared to grow out of the side of his head and curled down by the side of his ears and came to a point—much like a ram. His eyes were white with large dark black pupils. He appeared to be at ease and was talking to a white man in French. I speak fluent French, so I recognized his French was perfect. He would laugh occasionally. He, too, had a very melodious, soothing voice.

As they came to the end of their conversation, the Frenchman bowed and left the room. Gbezx and I sat down on a bench facing Lucifer about 30 feet from his throne. The Asian woman waiting at the end of our bench rose up in turn and went forward to meet him and began to speak to him in Japanese.

Gbezx and I were the last ones in the room, except for a couple of devils. I was very nervous. Gbezx sensing my discomfort, told me in a low voice to relax and that I would enjoy the experience of speaking with The Master. After about 15 minutes, the Asian woman gave a short bow and left.

So. I was next! Gbezx went up and spoke with him for a few minutes and then motioned me to come to stand by him. With my knees shaking, I went to face Lucifer. He studied me for a minute and then said;

"Welcome to the Underworld, Mr. Baker. Gbezx has told me you may be a good candidate to work for us in the Upper World."

As he spoke, I felt a strange calm come over me. He said he understood I had met his Four Horsemen.

"Yes," I said, "the one called Pestilence told me he was responsible for the COVID virus that has been causing so many deaths and financial hardships in our world."

"Yes, they have done great work for us and continue to do so. Let's get to the reason I summoned you here. Like the two other of our human agents you saw earlier, we have a network of humans who carry out a number of missions for us all over the world. As an example, a number of them coordinated with the Horseman we call War, and they were able to convince Putin in Russia to attack Ukraine. All this is very satisfying to me, as it shows our abilities how to foment hatred and distrust in your Upper World. This is the golden time of opportunity for us, as there hasn't been so much turmoil and confusion in hundreds of years in the Upper World."

"Our influence has been powerful in many countries. Kim Jong-un in North Korea is influenced by a number of our people in his military and political circles. We are planting the seeds for war between North Korea and Japan—which, of course, will bring in the Americans. China will move on to Taiwan. Russia will use strategic nuclear bombs against Ukraine, and the NATO nations will respond alike. China and the U.S. will launch attacks with intercontinental missiles. This, if our plans go as we have envisioned, will precipitate our long hoped-for nuclear world war."

Lucifer continued;

"After War will be Pestilence, Famine, and then Death. This is my time! Finally! After waiting for thousands of years for conditions to be just right. Many of your nations have nuclear bombs; Pakistan, India, North Korea, China, France, England, Israel, United States, Russia, and maybe others. I will have completed my goal to destroy the Upper World."

"I thought during your First and Second World Wars it was my time to make a move. My human agents advised me to wait. Through my agent governors, we will begin a new order directed by me. You, too, may have the opportunity to be one of the governors if you are diligent in your work for us. I'm thrilled with the unfolding events."

Lucifer told us we needed to leave now but that our conversation would continue later. One of the agents went before him, and they began conversing in German. Gbezx and I got up and left the room. I felt surprisingly energized and excited. Gbezx and I, with our escorts, continued along the path. We left using a different elevator than the one we came down on. The new elevator door opened, discharging an individual in a white turban who greeted Gbezx in a language I was not familiar with. I asked if he was from India, and he replied he was from Bangladesh.

We continued on as the hall began to zigzag back and forth. In the next room was a military-like formation consisting of maybe 500 devils with 100 or so winged devils in the rear. An apparent officer devil with a red sash across his shoulder was addressing them in their own strange language. The officer nodded his head toward Gbezx. I asked him what this was all about. He said they were in training for a future event.

Gbezx said that Lucifer had asked him to interview me to see if I would fit in. I asked him what exactly my service would entail. He explained I would start out in a smaller French-speaking country as;

"I believe you are more proficient in French. One of our agents was killed in an auto accident in Quebec, Canada. This was the official police report; however, we suspect foul play from our enemies. She was also a new agent and was not very careful—although, in time, she could have been very good. Your position would be as an investigative news reporter for a small paper we control. We continually need information on the city government and services. You will need to be very alert and close-mouthed about everything. You will be observed, trained, and also helped."

He went on to explain how they have agents in all the cities in the world.

"We have strong, very secretive enemies who are manned and financed through the major world churches. You will be instructed on how you may help our termination agency with its important work in combating them. Now, at this point, I must tell you this: If you decide not to join us, then you must remain here in Hades for the rest of your life. If you join us, then you will reside in the Upper World, you will be monitored, and you cannot escape our network. However, your work will be exciting and even more rewarding as you age. You will not lack money and will live a comfortable middle- class life as long as you serve us well."

"How did you come to pick me?" I asked Gbezx. "One of our agents is in the community service club that you belong to and told us about you… you had the right qualifications, were under 35 years of age, smart, and fluent in multiple languages. You were not religious, not married, had no children, and were ambitious."

Gbezx opened a heavy door to a room with about 100 humans working on computers. I sure didn't expect this. The temperature inside was a pleasant 72 degrees. I asked what they were doing, and Gbezx said they were connected with our agents in the Upper World. He pointed to a wall at the end of the room and explained that they live in comfortable apartments beyond the computer room. These are people who didn't want to be agents in the Upper World. They wanted to remain here, but they had to pass vigorous tests to stay to do so.

"So, Mr. Baker. What is your decision?" Gbezx asked me. "Well, I do have mixed emotions of worry, fear, and excitement. But I think I would like to try it out."

Gbezx said that would be a wise decision, but we needed to go back and talk to The Master first to get his thoughts and his affirmation. We retraced our steps back down the path to the room. Gbezx told the receptionist we needed to see The Master, and we were ushered right in. Lucifer was finishing a conversation with a large black man who was dressed in a colorful robe and skull cap. I guessed he was from Africa, but I didn't recognize the language they were speaking. He acknowledged us with a nod of his head and then left the room.

Gbezx walked up front and spoke for a little while and then motioned for me to come forward. Lucifer began speaking French to me in his rich, melodious voice. He said he was pleased I was going to join them. He announced he planned to send me to Quebec, Canada, as I speak both French and English. He said Gbezx would provide me with personal needs, instructions, housing, and contact information for the individual I will report to, etc.

Gbezx and I left and walked down the path for some distance and came to a room with a number of shelves that had all kinds of sundries, various personal items, and other supplies. Gbezx told the human clerk behind a large desk table in English we needed a small briefcase and suitcase. The clerk asked me for my pants, shirt, and shoe sizes. Another human clerk went down the aisle and started picking out my clothes—enough for one change. They laid it all out on the table, and I put them in the suitcase. They added toothpaste, a razor, and other personal care and hygiene items.

Gbezx instructed the clerk to bring me three thousand Canadian dollars. Another clerk came up and was told I needed ID, so he went to his desk and started creating it on a machine. Gbezx told him my name was David Carr and gave him an address in Montreal, Canada. I was all set. After we left, we walked to a different elevator. Gbezx said I would take this elevator and end up in a commercial building that they owned, where there were offices, meeting rooms, and apartments, and I would stay in one of them. Gbezx put his hand on my shoulder and told me that he knew I would do well and he would see me again when I came down to report.

First Mission:

Canada

Istepped in, sat down, and went up at a tremendous speed. When the door opened, I was met by a very attractive young woman about 30 years old. She said, "Je suis Silvia et vous etes David, nest-ce pas?"

I said, "Oui."

"Do you prefer to speak English or French?"

"English, please," I said. "Okay, follow me to your room."

The room was small but pleasant enough with a full bath. She told me to put my things away and then come downstairs as dinner would be served in 20 minutes. I sat down on the bed and let out a big breath, and wondered;

"Wow, what in the world have I gotten myself into? Is this all for real?!"

Downstairs in the dining room, five other people besides Silvia were already sitting at the table. Silvia introduced me around the table. The first person was Erik, who was their computer guy; second was Alice, a reporter whom I would work with; third was Bob, the security expert; fourth was Silvia's assistant Mary; and fifth was Abel, who was an all-around support guy who had been there the longest.

Silvia was the unit chief/control operator. The cook and housekeeper was Maria. I liked her immediately, as she asked how I wanted my steak cooked. The conversation was centering around some comments in the local paper about the Satanists, which is what they called us. The article warned readers to be aware of people asking unusual questions. There was to be a talk in two days at the local Catholic Church about the threat of the Anti-Christ's influence in politics and business circles. Silvia told Alice that she and I needed to attend. Bob informed me that he was trailing one of our enemies and knew his whereabouts.

They were saying how most churches and some government agencies had secret agents whose goal was to destroy us. Their organizations had been around for thousands of years. Silvia said that they had rumors that the Ancient Order of the Knights Templar was still active behind the scenes and was helping finance some of the church's activities. Wow, I thought, that is hard to believe! "Clear back to the time of the Crusades! Quebec is kind of a hotbed of anti-Satan groups," she said, "and we must be very careful of who may follow us and not get caught."

Maria served us all a nightcap of sherry as we chatted for a while longer. Alice told me breakfast was early, at 7 AM. I was tired, so I excused myself and went to bed. After a breakfast of eggs and bacon and lots of hot coffee, I thought maybe I made the right choice. I sat next to Alice, who was a tall thin redhead with green eyes. She had a pleasant personality and was chatty. She asked me about my background and profession, and I told her I was an aquatic biologist. She said she had worked for a detective agency before becoming a reporter for a small newspaper.

Silvia told Alice and me that there was a protest about some environmental concerns in the small town about 20 miles from us and that Abel would drive us to it. Silvia was a very matter-of-fact type of person and rarely smiled. She said to be alert to any of the protesters who could potentially be of service to us and who may not be religious. She said we needed to recruit some more informants that could be friendly to our cause. I asked about the Atheists and their group if they have one. Silvia said that we couldn't trust the Atheists, as they were infiltrated with anti-Satan people. Some time back, one of their agents was compromised, and she was lucky to have escaped and had to go back to the Underworld to be reassigned.

Everyone left the table, and Alice took me around to show me what different people did. In the living/work room, we joined Erik as he worked on the computers. He said he relayed messages from us and received them from the people I had seen in the Underworld. He was also in contact with other offices around the globe. His system was highly encrypted, and he was very careful. He had quite a dry sense of humor. Bob, the security guy, had a desk a few feet over from Erik's and took out a small pair of binoculars and a small caliber revolver, and left the building.

Mary, Silvia's assistant, told Alice and me that Abel was in the car, waiting to take us to the small town where the protest was to take place. We went out through the garage and got into the car, which was a beat-up, maybe ten-year-old, Toyota. I joked with Abel that he should trade in this "beater car" for a new one. He said they change cars about every three months and buy old ones in different colors so they wouldn't be so identifiable for security reasons.

We headed out of town through the busy morning traffic, drove about twenty miles through the pouring rain, and parked a few blocks away from where the protestors were marching. We got out of the car, put up our umbrellas, and soon caught up with the crowd. We counted about 50 protestors. They were chanting, "Save our air, close the plant." Apparently, there was a fertilizer plant on the outskirts of town where, when the wind conditions were just right, it would blow the fumes into the residential areas.

Alice went to one side of the group, and I to the other. I asked a young lady if she lived in town and experienced the bad smells. She said no, she was just visiting her cousin who did live here.

"Is she here?" I asked.

"No, she has a cold and doesn't want to be out in the rain."

I thanked her and then asked a young guy in his twenties, who was wearing a hoodie, the same question. He said he had heard about the happening from a friend who saw it on the Internet. I asked him if he knew anyone who lived in the town, and he said no. I asked why the people who don't live in the town are out in this terrible weather; he said because it was fun and you might meet a cool chick. I asked where they were going, and he said he thought they were going to city hall, where someone would probably give a speech.

I kind of ambled over to where Alice was talking to a middle-aged woman carrying a protest sign. I asked the woman if she lived here before the plant was built, and she said it was built just after the war when she was just a child. In a few minutes, we came to the courthouse and discovered a number of people left—so only maybe 30 protesters remained. People were milling around, and once the speaker didn't show up, the group broke up.

Alice said we need to get together when we get back and write a story on what we experienced, brief Silvia, and then Erik will send it down to the Underworld (Hades). We walked down the street to find Abel, who observed we looked like drowned rats! We were wet and cold—thankfully, the old car heater worked!

Back at base, we showered, changed clothes, and joined the rest for a few appetizers and an adult beverage. They wanted to know how our "adventure" went, and we told them how uneventful it was. Maria cooked a great dinner, and after some small talk, we all headed to bed. The next day Alice and I filled in what had transpired yesterday to Silvia and Erik. Abel invited me to go with him and Maria to get groceries and some other supplies. Silvia said we should have a better look outside as it was starting to snow. Abel offered to loan me a warm jacket until I got my own. I suspected he wanted me to go along so he would have help putting on snow chains if needed.

Abel got a phone call from Erik, who needed another two phones. Abel explained how they have no direct phone service as they buy disposable phones, and after certain calls, they throw them away. The snow was really coming down, and we were lucky we got our errands completed before we had to put on chains.

Back at base, Bob, the security guy, talked about how one of his paid contacts told him there was going to be a large number of church leaders, security people, and other anti-Lucifer people coming to town and how valuable it would be to identify some of them. He said we should put out the word that we will pay cash for good leads. He also added that he was trying to find out where they would meet. Silvia ordered her assistant Mary, Alice, Abel, and me to get out there and find any intel we could give to Bob.

Bob told me that since I was the newbie, he would give a few pointers on how to tail a suspect. For example, if you were after someone in a car, it was best to tail with two cars of a different color. One could follow for a while, then pull off, and the second car could move in to follow. One would also have to make sure to get the address when they stopped. Following on foot, you would have to walk on the other side of the street. If the suspect stopped and turned, you would have to turn, too. He also told me that it was best to have one or two different colored jackets or shirts and hats. If the suspect went into a store, we should wait. If they went out the back door, there was not much we could do. If they went into a hotel or apartment building, we should get the address so we could bring a car to wait in. Sometimes, we could pick up the chase the next morning.

Bob said he had a contact who had been molested by a Catholic priest when he was a choir boy. He had friends who were church members, and they told him there was going to be a large meeting of various people from all over Canada who wanted us destroyed at the Notre Dame de Quebec Cathedral-Basilica coming up soon.

"Do we have to assassinate any of their people?" I asked.

"Not unless it is a self-defense situation, as we don't want any publicity or to let them know to what extent we are monitoring them. We send the information down to the Under World, and they decide what actions to take. We also have special agents we don't know about who may come up to assess situations up here as the occasion arises."

Bob asked Silvia over to see if she wanted Alice to maybe nose around the big Cathedral and maybe attend services. Silvia thought that was a good idea and wanted me to tag along as well. She said the complex was very large and had many different rooms, one of which was where they had church business meetings. If we could conceal one of us in a closet or small office, it would be ideal. There were several tourist tours we could take to scope out hiding places. She asked Mary if she could find out the schedules of the tours and sign up one for her and Alice and me on another one. We needed to go during the day if we could.

After dinner, Silvia came over to me and asked if I would come to her room so we could talk. After a while, I tapped on her door, and she invited me in. She was in a light bathrobe, and she beckoned me over to sit next to her on her couch. She had a fantastic body. As I had mentioned before, she was very direct and a matter-of-fact type of person. She asked me how long it had been since I had sex. I said;

"Um, uh, isn't that a personal question?" She said,

"Yes, of course it is. Is that a problem?"

I asked how long it had been for her. She said it had been too long, but that NO man had really turned her on until I came along. She gave me a big, passionate kiss and then stood up, took me by the hand, and pulled me into her bedroom.

She told me to get undressed and get in bed and that she would be right with me. What choice did I have? She is my boss! She came back, joined me in bed, and we started making love in earnest. She was very passionate. When we were finished, she said, "Thank you," turned on her side, and went to sleep! So, I thought, *my work here is done, I guess.* I got dressed quietly, slipped out, and went upstairs to my room. Wow! I will have to think about all this.

The next morning, for breakfast, she acted as if nothing had happened between us. I waited in the workroom to see if Mary had found out about the tours to the Cathedral. The morning tour started at 9:30, and the evening at 2:00, she learned. Silvia said that Alice and I were to go on the morning tour, and she would go in the evening. Bob reminded us to try to break away from the group if we could and find out what room or rooms the big meeting would be in and how important it was if we could listen in. "Wear soft-sole shoes and move quietly. Take money for the tour and lunch," he said. Abel went down to get the car ready, and the three of us followed him down and got in.

We drove to the beautiful and imposing Basilica Cathedral, where Abel dropped us off at the curb. We joined the tour group of about twenty people who were milling about waiting. The tour director came out of the church with one of the priests, who greeted us and asked if it was our first visit. A few hands went up, and he said we welcome all faiths. He said we would be amazed at how opulent the buildings are.

The priest opened the big door for us all to go in. He was right—it was immense and beautiful. Alice told him she had heard there was a large meeting room and asked if we could see that, too. After he said of course we could, the priest then left us with the tour director to take over. We went from room to room and into various other beautiful buildings. At the last building, we were shown into the meeting room, which contained a large round table of at least 15 feet in diameter, with chairs surrounding it and another row of chairs against the walls. At one end, there appeared to be a staircase. Alice lagged behind the group as they went around the table, and when the director was looking the other way, she snuck up the stairs.

To stall some time, I asked the director some questions and positioned myself so that she would face me, with her back toward the stairs. In a few minutes, Alice came back down and joined us. I looked around to see if there were any more openings in the room but didn't see any.

That ended the tour, so we went out through the gardens, back to the front of the Cathedral, and walked down the street to where Abel had parked.

Back in the workroom, we briefed the others about what we had seen. Alice said that when she went up the stairs, the walkway was narrow with a banister that led to a small storage room with brooms and other cleaning supplies. She could see down from there directly into the meeting room. A few feet further on, she came to another room where she found two priests at their desks. They looked up in uncomfortable surprise and asked what she was doing there. She told them she was with the tour and was looking for the restroom. The priest told her to go back down the stairs and ask the tour guide where to find one she could use. She hurried down the stairs and joined me.

Everyone started talking at once, but Bob called us to order and said we needed to make sure the big meeting would be in the room. We would have to get a key to the door that goes out to the garden, and one of us would go up and hide in the utility room to watch and hear what was being said. Alice had said there were several large boxes one could hide behind in case someone looked in. This would, of course, be very dangerous. If we were caught, we could be tortured and killed.

The next day, Silvia went on the evening tour. She paid special attention to the meeting room, saw where the utility room was, and considered the chances of someone downstairs looking up to see it. She said there seemed to be a 50/50 chance of being spotted, so maybe our person could wear janitor-type clothes or possibly even wear a priest's frock.

Later the next day, Bob's sources reported that the first meeting was scheduled for the evening in two days. Silvia asked if the key and clothing would be ready. To be fair, she said we should draw straws to see who would act as a spy.

Silvia went to the kitchen and brought back three sticks of spaghetti. She had Bob pull the first one, Alice next, and me last. Of course, you guessed it, I got the short stick. I wasn't pleased, but I thought to myself, well, you can't live forever. Silvia suggested I go back to the church and take the evening tour, as there would be a different tour guide and hopefully a new group of tourists.

Knights Templar

Returning to the church that evening, there were only six people. When no one was looking, I snuck up the stairs, went into the little room, and saw it was as Alice had described. I came back down quickly and re-joined the others.

The following evening, Bob produced the key to the meeting room, and Mary had found a set of bib overalls closely matching what church's janitors wore and a soft fabric hat. We were as ready as we could be.

The second evening, when the meeting was to take place at the church, I put on my Janitor clothes and floppy hat. Everyone wished me well as I rode off with Abel to the side of the church. I had the key to the side door and hustled up and opened it. Just as I went in, I heard voices coming from the inside hallway leading to the meeting room. *Oh crap*, I thought as I hurried up the stairs and into the janitor's closet, cracking the door just enough to peer into the meeting room below.

What happened next was at once fascinating and frightening. Entering the room were two priests, who then stood aside while twelve Knights Templar entered in full armor. They all wore chain mail, even on their heads like a hoodie. Their helmets were round and went up to a sharp top. Their shields were about five feet tall, flat on top, and came down to a point at the bottom. Red Maltese Crosses were painted on them. On their backs, they had a scabbard that held a long two-sided sword with a two-foot hilt. Steel breastplates were worn over the chain mail.

They circled the table until they all stood behind a massive, heavy chair. They each placed their shield on the table, with the pointed bottom end facing the center of the table. Standing behind them, the priest said something in Latin, which apparently ordered the Knights to pull their long swords from the scabbards on their backs. They all kneeled down on one knee, placed the sword tips on the floor, and then gripped their sword hilts with both hands.

The Knights all bowed their heads as the priest began a prayer in Latin. Rising as one, they got up and arranged the tips of the swords together at the center of the table. In unison, they all began to speak in what sounded like old English. I caught a few words and parts of a sentence here and there. "We are soldiers of Christ; we are just and good; our Order is old and sacred; we spill the blood of our enemies; our bodies are strong," and other similar phrases. After continuing for maybe fifteen or twenty minutes, they holstered their swords and bent down on one knee again while the other priest gave another prayer. After concluding, the Knights lifted their shields from the table, put their arms through the grips, and silently filed out of the room following the priests.

Stunned, I went down on my knees and sucked in the air till I got my breath back with some deep breathing. Once I had calmed down, I pondered what I had learned and what kind of useful information I could report.

To be safe, I waited for about an hour and then went gingerly down the stairs. Hearing no talking or noise, I slipped quietly out the back door and walked down the street looking for Abel. My heart skipped a beat or two when a car pulled up beside me, and a lady asked me if I needed a ride. I was so nervous that I barely mumbled, "Thanks, but I live close by." The lady drove off, much to my relief, but I wondered how much more excitement I could handle today!

After walking a couple of more blocks, I spotted Abel's car just ahead. I stopped next to a tree, and as I had been instructed, I looked back, across the street, and up ahead in case anyone was watching the car. The coast was clear, so I knocked on the window, waking Abel, got in the car, and let out a very big sigh of relief.

Abel wanted to know how it went, but I said I'd wait till we got back as I needed to rest a bit and collect my thoughts.

Over breakfast the next morning, I relayed my adventures from the day before to the group. There were, of course, many questions and comments. Erik, the computer guy, asked me to join him at his computer so he could send my story down to the Underworld. Bob, the security guy, said he was going out to meet with his contact from the church who had been molested by the priest and was very helpful with inside information. He wanted to get some feedback from me about my experience. Erik, Silvia, and I waited for two hours for a response.

A message started coming through from Gbezx, my old guide. He complimented me and said that Lucifer was very pleased. He asked that we double our effort to obtain more information on the Knights - who they were and where they lived.

Lucifer said a few of them had shown up in different parts of the globe, and they were disruptive to some of our projects. They appeared to have a very strong religious zeal and were extremely secretive. They also seemed to have unlimited funds, which I thought were most likely plunder from some of their quests in the Middle East.

"Keep up the good work, and let us know if you need anything," he said as they signed off.

Silvia told Alice and me to take some flyers she had obtained from an Atheist group that was handing them out on street corners. She instructed us to go to the high schools, junior colleges, and the university and put them in the libraries and lunch rooms—wherever the students gathered. She said to remember where we left them and go back tomorrow and see how many were remaining and to replace them if gone. There were probably 500 flyers, and they stated the usual anti-Christ message with a phone number to call. Abel took us to a number of schools, and we stopped for lunch at an on-campus McDonald's.

We spent the rest of the day circulating flyers. After running out of flyers, we planned to come back the next day. At one trade school, an instructor picked up one of the flyers and started yelling at us—calling us dirty devil worshippers and using a string of curse words; he chased us out. Alice was a little shaken up, but Abel calmed her by saying that it was not a normal incident. He recommended we should be careful where we place the flyers and avoid placing them when people might be around to observe us.

Back home, Maria prepared some thick juicy steaks, complete with a wonderful Caesar salad and baked potato with slabs of butter, sour cream with chives—the works. The group seemed to have plenty of money, so we ate really well. Bob reported back that his church contact had some information on the Knights and that we would meet with him the next day.

Later that evening, Silvia gave me a nod towards her room. I guess she was feeling romantic. I waited a while, reading a newspaper until everyone else had left, and went into her room. She was already in bed, so I undressed and joined her. She said nothing, and when we finished, it was just like the first night. She rolled over and went to sleep.

The next morning, Mary, Silvia's assistant, went with me to hand out flyers as Alice was still a little upset. We went to the big university with all the flyers in an open-topped briefcase. As we walked around, we left only a few at a time.

As we walked around, we came to a group of students who were talking about the pros and cons of socialism. We sat down next to them, and I asked one of the students what side she was on.

She said, "I don't like the way the wealthy have all that money and don't help the poor out more, but I'm not sure all of their ideas are really that good. Someone has to work."

I asked her if she thought the churches had too much money.

She said, "Yes. Instead of building those big Cathedrals, they could build housing for the poor."

I asked if she paid her own tuition, and she said she had a grant from some large fund. When I asked where the fund got their money, she replied, "I don't know. Maybe from the President or the government. Are you a reporter or something?"

I told her I was a news reporter and that it was nice talking to her. The bell rang, and the students got up and went to their classes.

That evening, we all relayed our day's experiences and compared notes. Mary was exceptionally good at talking and asking questions of people. Bob had spoken to his church contact, who gave him the story of the Knights.

"Not unlike the Catholic Church's Knights of Columbus and other groups within groups, they are local businessmen— accountants, realtors, attorneys, etc.—and, of course, all very religious. The Knights of Columbus Order is in every Catholic Church in the world, but the Knights Templar is a separate Order and won't be. The Knights Templar are much more aggressive and have been known to attack, torture, and even kill Satanists. The contact didn't have any personal information on the Templars as they are extremely cautious and secretive and deliberately invisible so they can melt back into society.

That evening, I asked Bob why all the agents like him didn't just leave and go to a different country or somewhere.

He said, "All of us, including you, have a tracking implant that you probably didn't even realize when it was inserted. After several years of good service, you can petition to have it removed. They know where everyone is in the world."

I picked up the local newspaper, *the Le Journal de Montreal*, off the table, sat back in one of the recliners, and saw articles about the Ukrainians and Russians fighting, Putin saber rattling, North Korea firing missiles, unrest in Iran, worries about Taiwan and China, looming winter fuel shortages in Europe, food shortages, COVID, world weather catastrophes, etc. I thought back to what the Four Horseman of the Apocalypse had told me: *Pestilence, War, Famine, and Death.* All of these were currently at play in the world. Like all of the rest of us, all we could do was plan as much as we could and let the world events unfold as they would.

Lucifer had his plans and was hoping for a worldwide nuclear war so he could dominate—and all he had to do was to let us destroy each other so he could come pick up the pieces. There really was not much more to be said except that you pick your leaders wisely.

That evening, we got a call from Gbezx. He told Erik to have me come back down to the Underworld as soon as possible. He said I would be going on a new temporary assignment, so it was best for me to take all my possessions with me. I loaded up my suitcase, gave everyone a big hug, and with an assurance I would be back, said my goodbyes, stepped into the elevator and ended up back in Hades. In a few minutes, Gbezx met me and said we would go directly to see the Master. We were ushered in. A woman was speaking some Scandinavian language and, after a short conversation, bowed and then left the room. Lucifer asked me in his deep, melodious voice,

"Hablas Español?"

"Si," I replied. Speaking Spanish.

He congratulated me on my adventure with The Templar Knights and said I was clever and lucky. He started with, "After the Second World War, a number of the Nazis came to Argentina, and we were able to convert a number of them to our side. Their offspring also joined our ranks as the older ones died. The Jews had been vigorously pursuing them, as well as the Catholics and other church groups. A number of them had been assassinated and their land and possessions confiscated. We now had a situation where one of the high-ranking officials of the Argentine Government was causing us grief."

I was listening intently.

Lucifer then continued,

"The guy has been one of our people for many years and knows a lot of our agents, safehouses and methods and is attempting to blackmail us and is asking for millions of dollars. We know he has covered his trail well; however, he will be at a big government meeting in two weeks in Buenos Aires. There is only one solution to this problem: he must be assassinated. Gbezx and I have come to the conclusion that you have the resourcefulness, courage, and smarts to pull off this dangerous mission to a satisfactory close. We have a very good agent who is in an ultra-secret agency, the KGB, in Russia. We would like you to go there, and he can train you in methods he has perfected to eliminate undesirable people with no trace of injury. We understand this will be very risky for you. You will be rewarded handsomely."

Lucifer then took a break and, after looking at me and smiling, said, "What are your thoughts about taking a human's life? Keep in mind this person is a traitor, and will endanger many of our people, and doesn't deserve to live. Gbezx, why don't you take Senior Carr to your office, and the two of you can talk it over."

We left the throne room and went out onto the path. Gbezx called over two large, winged devils. They bent down and Gbezx climbed aboard one and told me to do the same. He said to hold on tight and lean forward. He said his office was a way down the path from here, so we would have to take a quicker method of getting there. My devil flapped his wings very fast and up we went and down the hall. It was kind of fun. In maybe fifteen minutes, we stopped and dismounted. There was a devil guard with a trident in front of a closed door that the devil pushed open and we went inside. I was totally blown away. The room was about 50 x 100 feet with a 20-foot ceiling that crystal chandeliers hung from. The walls were covered with antique art, Titans, Rubens, Raphael, Leonardo Da Vinci, Van Gogh, Monet, Vermeer and many more. The room was filled with beautiful antique furniture and rugs.

Gbezx said, "I see you like art."

"Yes. I love it!" I said. He walked over to this huge, finely carved wood desk and motioned to me to sit down in a wonderful, upholstered chair across from it and he sat down behind the desk. He said he had collected for hundreds of years. To the right of my chair was a large old treasure box full of thousands of gold coins. I asked if it was a pirate's hoard. Yes, it was just part of Blackbeard's treasure. "Where's the rest," I asked.

He added, "It is in our large depository as well as millions of other valuables. We have more gold than your Fort Knox. We use these assets to fund our operations around the Upper World."

Gbezx then started talking business, "Now, let's talk about the assignment the Master proposed to you. What do you think about taking on this challenge?"

"Well, I don't know," I said.

Operation Russia

Gbezx then continued, "As an inducement, since you like antiques, I could arrange for a nice room for you to stay in when you visit us here, and you could go to the Depository and pick out what art and furniture you would desire to furnish it. You would also have a higher rank over the devils, so you can move around unimpeded while you are here. You will wear a special uniform. You will only answer to me and the Master. This is how important this mission is."

"Please tell me a little bit more about the plan," I asked.

"Okay, you will meet with, we will call Boris, a high-ranking KGB officer. He will take the lead and arrange your secure housing, etc. He will train you in his secret methods on what to do and how to do it. He will be with you in Argentina to guide you as the Master said it is very dangerous there now for us. Boris speaks fluent Spanish, so you will have no problems communicating. You must commit now as we can't have you changing your mind. I'm going to leave you now for a little while so you can think about this. I have confidence in you as you have proved yourself in Canada." With that, he got up and left the room.

Well, I thought, *what kind of dangerous mess have I got myself into now? Do I really want to be an assassin? If I was successful, would they want me to do more? How can I get out of this dilemma? The positives would be I would have some bearing and status here and have fun with their priceless antiques. It could be very exciting. I could get killed. (If I did, I guess I would end up here anyway?) This is so unreal it is hard to imagine. What to do, what to do?*

After a while Gbezx came back into the room.

"Well, what have you decided?" he asked.

"I guess I have some morality issues. I was raised not to harm my fellow man, to be of good cheer, to work hard and obey the law. I just never considered taking another's life."

Gbezx then told me things I didn't know, "You need to consider this, David. Our person of interest, Ruben Covarrubias, is the Ministro de Turismo in Argentina. He makes a fortune from kickbacks from most of the cruise ship lines and travel groups. He is a very corrupt individual. We have no problem with what he does if he doesn't harm us. This is why we are so surprised about his ransom demands, as we know he is probably the richest man in South America. Rumor has it he wants to be president and it will require a fortune in payoffs as he has such a bad reputation. You are eliminating our enemy as well as providing a good service to their people. Let's do this. You go to Moscow and train with (we shall call him Boris). If you decide you just can't pull it off, then we will bring you back for a different assignment. No harm done. Now, however, I do need you to be pretty well committed before we waste more time because we have a short time frame to act."

"Well, if you give me a fair chance to back out when I have a panic attack, then let us proceed," I said.

"I think you will be fine," Gbezx said. "We will need to go back to the supply room, get you set up for Russia with a new ID, etc. Your new name will be Jorge Carrillo," he added. Gbezx called over the two large winged devils, which we mounted and ended up in the supply room again. I was given Russian clothes, boots, a new ID, and two thousand rubles. On our way to the elevator, Gbezx said that I would end up in the back room of an old warehouse that had double doors. I would have to wait in between the doors, and one of Boris's people would come and get me. He also warned me not to speak to anyone except Boris. They had sent him my bio and he was anxious to meet me. We came to the elevator.

Gbezx put his claw on my shoulder and said, "I know you will be fine. Boris will communicate with us on a regular basis." With that, he pushed the up button and away I went. I ended up in this chamber with a large steel door. I sat down on a narrow shelf and waited.

In about thirty minutes, the door squeaked open. A tall, attractive blond of about 35 came into the room. She motioned me to follow her. We went through a series of doors and to a waiting black car with dark-tinted windows. I got in the back and the blond got in the driver's seat and we drove through a metal overhead door. We drove for about an hour without speaking and came to this large farmhouse out in the country. She drove around to the back and an automated door opened and we went in. A 6-foot man of about 55 came forward to greet me. He said, "Como sta Jorge, I'm Boris." I said the same to him.

We went into the house's living room, which was full of Radios, computers and other electronics, and a number of operators who were monitoring them. I followed Boris past the kitchen down the hall to an office room. He went behind a desk and asked me to take a seat across from him. He asked how my trip was and went on to say he had never been to Hades and wanted to go some time. It was a little difficult to understand some of the Spanish words he was speaking because they were either Valencian or Castilian Spanish. I told him I was taught Mexican Spanish, not the classics he spoke, so we both spoke slower and the more we spoke, the easier it got.

He said that he had some ideas on how to achieve our mission.

He reached into his desk and pulled out a ring. He twisted the ring, and a very small needle appeared. He said that it contained a very powerful poison and would kill in about 30 to 45 minutes after injection. He turned it again and the needle disappeared. It would work if I simply touched the person on the arm or anywhere else. He also said that they wouldn't even feel anything, at most, a small pin prick. He put it on my finger and it fitted fine. He took the ring off and put it in a small case. He said, "Obviously, you need to use it with great caution. Here is my idea: the Ministro and his aids will be attending an important meeting with other Government officials. Our contacts have sent us a floor plan and approximate times they will arrive at the building. We arrange to follow the Ministro and his aids as they walk down the hall to the conference room. You close up on them and say, 'Senior Ministro. I am a representative of Viking Cruise Lines and we want to do business with you.' He will probably stop and then you can shake his right hand and with your left hand, you clasp his left arm and inject him. You give him a fake business card and ask him to call you. I will be behind you, so turn and follow me down the hall quickly."

He pulled out the floor plans and we looked over them carefully. We had a flight leaving Moscow in two hours for Buenos Aires. We also have side-by-side seats in 1st class. Our passports were ready and we had Viking cruise ship brochures to show the customs people why we were there. We wouldn't have any problems with the Russians.

After a long flight, we arrived at Buenos Aries Aeroporto. Boris gave me a card with the hotel address we would stay at. He said we would need to take separate taxis to the hotel for security reasons. He said that he would wait fifteen or twenty minutes and then he would come. After breakfast tomorrow morning, we would go to the government building and scope it out. We went to the building at 9 AM when it opened and walked to the floor where we would be the next day. It looked like what we had planned. Boris asked me how I was doing. I told him I felt more confident and was not so nervous. The next morning, Boris was going to wait outside and watch for the Minestro's limousine to arrive and I would wait in the hallway and sit in one of the chairs that lined the walls, and then Boris would come ahead of the others and alert me.

At about 10 AM, Boris came walking past me, and I stood up and waited for the men to go ahead of me and then started to walk. At that time, three men came up and pushed me out of the way and one of them shot the Minestro in the back of his head. All three ran back down the hall, shot one of the security officers, and quickly made their exit. *Holy crap*, I thought, *did this really happen?* Boris motioned to me to leave and to follow him. We went to the street and then hailed a cab and went back to the hotel.

We went to the Hotel bar and ordered a drink. Boris said he saw in an old American movie once where one of the characters ordered three fingers of red whiskey. He said I feel like having one now, so we both ordered one instead of vodka for him and a beer for me. After this last experience, it was harsh, but it hit the spot. I asked Boris if the hit on the commissioner was ordered by Gbezx as a backup plan in case I wasn't able to pull it off. He said he didn't think so, and he had a call with his contact there to see if they had found anything out. The incident was all over the news. We sipped our whiskeys in silence for a while and then we went to our rooms for the night. The next morning, during breakfast, Boris got a call from his contact, who said the rumor was that one of the cruise lines that had paid the Ministro a lot of money for docking privileges got moved to an undesirable berth in a bad location. They tried to work out something with the commission, but they had cut a more lucrative deal with another cruise line. It was all about the money. After hanging up, Boris said;

"I guess it doesn't matter who killed him; the job is done. The only negative for you and I is we may not get our bonus."

"Yeah, I have been thinking about that too," I said.

He then continued talking, "I think we better get back to Moscow as soon as we can and report the situation." We were lucky and got a flight that was about to leave in 2 hours. The trip back was uneventful.

We arrived in Moscow and the tall, blonde, unsmiling woman picked us up and she drove with Boris and I in the back. I asked her what her name was. Boris said she was mute and didn't hear well. Her name was Natalia. I asked Boris what she did for his organization. He said she did a lot of odd jobs and was good on the computer.

I said, "Too bad about her condition."

"Yes," he said. "Too bad."

Boris and I went to the computer, and after a while, Gbezx came online. Boris and I explained the events in Argentina to him. Gbezx had a lot of questions, of course, and he told me to come back to the Underworld now and inform the Master in person. So, I gathered my things and said my goodbyes. Boris said he enjoyed working with me and maybe our paths would cross again sometime. Boris walked me to the elevator; I went in, pushed the red button and down I went. Gbezx met me and said the Master wanted to see me in his office. We hitched a ride on two of the big, winged devils and they took us to the Master's office. The devil guard on the door went inside and in about five minutes, came back out and motioned us in. The room was about the same size as Gbezx's and again furnished with lavish furniture and wall hangings. Lucifer was sitting on a beautiful, massive-carved desk. He got up and came around to greet me. He was at least eight feet tall. He put out his claw-like fist and said, "Isn't it common practice in the upper world to fist bump?"

Wow, I thought, *fist-bumping with the devil!!* A shiver went up my back. Lucifer tilted back his head and laughed; I'm sure sensing my feelings. He went back to his desk. There were multiple TV and computer screens on the side of his desk.

He motioned for Gbezx and me to sit down on the beautiful stuffed chairs. He said, speaking in Spanish, "So I will continue to call you Jorge until you go to a different country. Tell us your story of what happened. Have they verified the assassins were hired by the Cruise company? Well, we have our people working on that now. It wasn't any of our operatives, I can assure you."

I started telling the whole story, and both of them asked a lot of questions. When I came to the end, Lucifer said Gbezx asked me if I had doubts and bad feelings about me performing the assassination. Yes, I said. I told him it was kind of against my nature and I was quite fearful I couldn't pull it off.

Lucifer said, "We will never know now, will we?"

"No, I guess not," I said.

"Our goal," Gbezx said, "was to eliminate the traitor. And that was accomplished no matter who did it."

Lucifer said, "You did well in spite of it all. Boris said he enjoyed working with you. I believe that Gbezx will have another mission for you so I will let you go."

Gbezx and I rose and left the room.

The Disappearance of Bob

Gbezx said, "I'm going to send you back to Quebec. Bob, the security guy you worked with before, has been missing for three days and we don't have any leads. Do you need any more clothes, personal items, or money?" I didn't spend any money the last time I was there, and I was okay otherwise. He also added, "You should ask Alice to take you shopping as she loves to shop, Silvia tells me."

We went back to his office and he called Silvia to let her know I was coming. "She was happy to hear you are coming back," he said. The door to the elevator was close by, so we walked down the path, opened the door, got in and then I bid Gbezx goodbye. I was soon in Quebec.

Silvia was waiting in the transport room; the inner door was closed and she gave me a big kiss and said she was feeling romantic, so she invited me to her room. We went through the outer door and went around greeting the others. Erick, the computer guy, gave me a fist bump. He is a short, portly man in his middle forties and he was born in Quebec. Mary, Silvia's assistant, gave me a big hug as well. She was a tall woman with long black hair in her fifties and was born in Ottawa. I got another hug from Alice, the other reporter. She is of average height, has red hair with freckles and has a cute face. She was born in Montreal. I would guess she is in her late twenties. Abel, the all-around support guy, was a muscular 6-foot about 35-year-old who was bald and gave me a fist bump. He was also born in Quebec. Maria, the cook, was in the kitchen. She was a plump, dark-haired, middle-aged woman who was born in Honduras.

Silvia said, "Well, David, you are turning out to be quite a Super Star. You hobnob with Lucifer and Gbezx and travel around the world on exciting adventures. Where did you go?"

I said, "I'm sorry, but I can't reveal my whereabouts. I'm sure you understand."

I suggested we all sit down at the dining room table and do some brainstorming about Bob's disappearance. Mary provided us all with yellow pads and pencils. I asked what Bob was doing and if he met someone before he left the other day. Erik said he had a contact he was trying to recruit and was also following a suspect agent of the church. We also located his car, which was just a few blocks from the church you saw the Templar Knights in. We did not pick up the car for fear it might be watched.

"Was there any ID or file in it?" I asked.

Silvia said we didn't register the cars in our name and we took the license plates off another car in a different city. We left no papers or ID in the car. We paid cash to a used car dealer who bent the rules for us. There was a note on Bob's desk with a name on it and a time and date from a week ago, just before he disappeared. I asked if they thought Bob would break under torture. Silvia said he had an arsenic pill he carried and she believed he would swallow it before being questioned. Silvia said if they did break Bob, you would think their agents would be here by now. I said since the car was not too far from the church, maybe we should pay another visit to their next open house like Alice and I did before.

"Do we know how to contact the person Bob was trying to recruit," I asked.

Erik said that might be dangerous as the recruit may be playing both sides and could have set Bob up.

Silvia said it appears that this Louie is our best lead and David and Alice can go nose around. Silvia asked Mary to find out the times of their next tours through the church.

Maria brought us all a glass of Sherry, and we all went into the living room so Maria could set the table for dinner and we all started chatting about ideas to find this Louie guy.

Maria had cooked up a nice rack of lamb and a good-tasting vegetable dish. Erik opened a vintage bottle of wine, which was excellent. After a while, everyone started heading off to bed. Silvia winked at me and headed to her room.

I went to my room and waited till everyone had gone to their room. I then went up to Silvia's room. She was already in bed. I got undressed and joined her. She was very passionate, and the lovemaking was very enjoyable. She said it was the best sex she had ever experienced. I said thank you, and it was good for me too. I got dressed and left for my room as quietly as I could.

The next morning, we had a breakfast of eggs, baked tomatoes, potatoes, bacon or sausage, and rolls with orange marmalade. Delicious!

Mary said there was going to be a church tour today at 10 AM. Abel said about 9:45, he would have the car ready. Alice and I got in the old car that Abel had bought from the dealer the day before, and let us off about six blocks away from the church.

We walked in with about fifteen others. As the group was walking to the next room, Alice asked the Pastor if she knew a man called Louie, who she thought was a member of the congregation. Alice explained she had borrowed some money from him and wanted to pay him back. The Pastor said he didn't know him, but if she came back this evening, he would ask around. She would need to come to his office on the second floor, which was just down the walkway from where I had hidden in a closet from the Templar Knights sometime before.

Alice had knocked on their door and the priests asked what she wanted and she told them she was looking for the restroom. In a gruff voice, they told her downstairs. We followed the group and then left and walked down the street for about six or seven blocks to where Abel was waiting for us.

When we got back, Alice told everyone what the Pastor had told her. Everyone at once started talking and saying it sounded like a trap! Although Alice was wearing dark glasses and a head covering, it would not be wise for her to go back as we believed they had security cameras. We decided I shouldn't go back either. We knew we should act as quickly as we could to try to rescue Bob from torture. We talked for some time.

Abel suggested we get rid of the car and trade it back to the unscrupulous used car dealer for another different colored old car. Silvia agreed and Abel left to do the swap. I got to thinking to myself that maybe we had better get help from Gbezx. Maybe have Boris and his specialists come to make a fresh start. I'm sure they have KGB contacts here who could help. I got Silvia aside and told her my thoughts. She said it sounds good, but we don't want Gbezx to think we are incompetent. She said she wanted to think it over a bit. Erik, Alice, Mary and I continued to chat about our predicament in the living room over a nice couple of bottles of wine that Erik had procured from a wine shop downtown Quebec.

After a while, Silvia came over and joined us, and Erik gave her a glass. She said David had an idea and that it might be wise to contact Gbezx and tell him about our dilemma. David knows a Russian KGB officer he has worked with before who may be able to help us. We decided to contact Gbezx as we are really limited and more or less surrounded by potential enemies, and we don't have Bob's help.

So we all followed Erik over to the communication device and called Gbezx. After a brief wait, Gbezx came on. We told him everything that had happened and our worries about blowing our cover. I told him my thoughts on maybe Boris and his undercover agents could step in. After a few more questions, Gbezx said he would consult with the Master and call us back.

The next day, at about noon, Gbezx called back. He said the Master was very upset and worried that our location here may be compromised. Gbezx said that the Master wanted us to do the following:

"Alice goes around the back entrance, walks down the alley for a couple of blocks, comes to the front, and starts walking down the street. She needs to have a front pack on with a doll in it and maybe carry a diaper bag. After a while, Erik needs to follow her after she has walked two or three blocks, watching very carefully to see if someone in a car or walking is watching her. He needs to carry an empty suitcase. David needs to do the same, following Erik. David needs to have a camera around his neck and take fake pictures pretending he is a tourist. All of you need to take a small pair of powerful binoculars. Abel can pick up all these items when he goes shopping. Abel needs to park in the parking lot, go through the store and out the back door quickly, and come to the front and see if anyone is watching the car. I know you are going to a number of different stores in various areas. You need to do this for the next three days, taking different items, changing the order of who goes first, wearing different clothes and hats, etc.

"We are working on a team to come to assist you. You need to buy a cheap throw-away phone. I will call you for the number in a few days. A French-speaking woman, who is the leader of a team, will call David for a meeting, and he would have to cross the street so they can watch you before the meeting.

The instructions went further. "David, you will need to get as much information as you can. She will not know your location or limited data about you. She is a very matter-of-fact and serious type of person. Her name is Violette."

A few days later, Gbezx called us for the phone number and to alert us that Violette would be calling real soon. In an hour, Violette was on the phone. She said she would like to talk to Silvia and me at a house out of town. She said to go to the corner of 5th and Fairmont streets, which was about five blocks away, and a grey car would pick us up then at 6 PM. According to her, I needed to wear a green bill cap and Silvia a yellow scarf. The next day, we started walking to the location, and one of us would turn occasionally and look back. At 6 PM sharp, a grey car pulled over and we boarded quickly. The driver melted in with rush hour traffic and we headed out of town. Our driver was a blond-headed young lady who said we could call her Suzette. We made small talk about the terrible traffic and the cold weather. She said it was about an hour's drive and there were water bottles in the back for us. From Quebec, we drove North through Saquenaye and out into the countryside and to a gravel road. We came to an old frame farmhouse with a barn, some outbuildings and some cattle grazing in a pasture. A woman in a warm-looking hooded jacket came out of the door of the house and opened two doors to the garage, and we drove in. The woman then closed the doors and introduced herself as Michelle.

We were ushered in and met Violette, who was a striking, beautiful young woman. She reminded me of the old movie star Grace Kelly. I thought to myself, *I will have a hard time keeping my eyes off her.*

Michelle invited us to the kitchen, and we all sat down at the table. Suzette served us hot chocolate, which really hit the spot. The old kitchen looked original but was clean and large. It even had an old wood-fired cookstove.

Violette asked how our trip was and Suzette complained about the traffic. Violette said it was a good thing as a tail would have a very difficult time trying to follow us. After our hot chocolates, we went into a large living room furnished with antique couches, chairs, tables and a grand piano. Very charming. Silvia and I sat on a big, old, comfortable Davenport, and Violette sat across from us in a stuffed chair. Silvia and I told Violette the entire story, from our adventures with the Templar Knights, the Church, and everything going up to that time. She asked a lot of questions about Bob's habits and movements, who he knew, and any other names he might have mentioned. Silvia said they searched his room, his desk, and his clothes. His revolver was missing, but he usually took it with him. Silvia told Violette that Bob had a cyanide tablet he always carried in case he got captured. Violette said since we were not raided, she would guess he must have taken it. Too bad, yes, we said, too bad.

In about two hours, Michelle announced that dinner was ready. Suzette and Michelle had cooked a wonderful salmon dinner with an assortment of vegetables and warm bread. I said we were lucky to have French Chefs, and they both just smiled. We were served some wonderful French wine and a Sherry after with dessert. Violette said, "It is too late to go back tonight, so you can sleep here."

The guest bedroom has two single beds and the bathroom is down the hall, and the rooms have robes. So, we all said good night and we went to our room. Silvia said we had better behave ourselves tonight, and she said that she had seen me eyeing Violette! All I said was, "Well, she is very pretty." The next day, at breakfast of some wonderful crepes, Violette said, "When we get back to your building, we should lay low and not go out. Suzette would stop at a grocery store so you could stock up on some food." So, after goodbyes, we got in the car, which was different than the one we had come in. Since it was Saturday, the traffic was lighter, and we made better time and stopped at a store and bought groceries. When we got to our place, we went around the back alley. Erik and Abel helped us unload. Suzette drove away immediately.

Inside, we contacted Gbezx and brought him up to date. He said that Violette and her team were contract agents with them and were very good at their job. He also warned us not to leave the house for the next three or four days. He added, "Write down all the things that have happened. See if you can find out if Bob has relatives or friends that he may have contacted. If you find any, try to verify their validity, but don't try to contact them. If you do find more, let me know and I will inform Violette."

Alice and I combed through all of Bob's files and his desk and we found a small black book with some names and addresses. One had the same last name as Bob's, had a phone number that was disconnected and had an address in Eugene, Oregon. We checked some other old entries with our search engines. Alice said she thought Bob might have had a girlfriend as he had mentioned to her that he was going out with Barbara for dinner. We did find a Barbara in his black book with a phone number. We shared what we had found with Gbezx; he was pleased and asked that we keep digging. He said he would share our findings with Violette. He said he thought that we should be able to leave the building and use the same caution as we did before. He was curious about what happened to the old car we had left close to the Church. Erik looked up police reports on stolen cars, and it appears the car was stolen. It was also involved in a robbery and was wrecked in a police car chase. Ah, Gbezx said, that's a fitting end for it. He asked Silvia what her thoughts were of Mary and her going to the Church and maybe attending a few services.

Gbezx said assertively, "You will both need to wear Christian crosses and, of course, cover your heads."

Both ladies said, "Yes, no problem, we can go to evening mass tomorrow."

Sacred Secrets

The next day, our support guy, Abel, was at a local hardware store getting some washers for a leaking faucet, and a young man came up to him and said, "Aren't you Bob's friend?" Abel was shocked and mumbled a meek, "How did you know?" The young man had a vest on. It had the name of the store and his name, Stewart, written on a name tag.

He introduced himself and said he recognized Abel as he was with Bob some time ago. He said that he had some information since he gathered work for Bob. He said he was the one who had been molested by one of the Priests. Abel said he knew him through Bob but didn't remember him. Stewart told Abel he hadn't seen Bob for some time. Wow, Abel thought. He was confused about how much he should tell the guy. *Well, what do I have to lose? This could be a break for us*, thought Abel.

Abel said, "I may have bad news for you. Bob has not been seen for over a week and we fear he may have been taken by the Church people. We don't know whether he is dead or alive."

"Man, that is really bad news," Stewart said. Since Bob paid him every week for his help, it was bad for him too. Plus, Stewart had to provide for his invalid mother and didn't make enough as a clerk in this store. Abel asked Stewart if he had any news for us. Stewart said that he had befriended another Church member who was a janitor in the Church. The janitor had told him he would nose around to find out about Bob. The janitor also said that he knew the Church members still had secret meetings in that room where Dave saw the Templar Knights. Abel gave Stewart a hundred Canadian dollars and told Stewart he would come to the hardware store occasionally and that he really needed to dig up some fresh information.

That evening, Abel shared what he had learned from Stewart, and we all thought that was a fortunate encounter. Abel drove Silvia and Mary to the Church and parked about six blocks west. He told them he would pick them up about six blocks the other way east at 9:30 PM after mass, and if they had to get picked up earlier, they would have to call. Silvia and Mary entered the Church and one of the priests came over to greet them in a friendly

manner and started to ask them questions. Those included why they came by, if they were Catholic, whether they had been there before, where they lived, etc. He took them over to a pew in the back. There were a lot of worshipers. They followed the rest through prayers, kneeling, and so on. Mary told Silvia she felt really nervous and Silvia said she was too.

They discussed if they should just leave or go up to the front where others were going. "Well, we haven't accomplished anything; we might as well leave," one of them said. They walked out with others leaving and started up the street, went behind a large tree and looked back. One of the priests and another man came hurrying out and were looking both ways, obviously looking for them. Silvia called Abel and told him about their dilemma. He said he was about two blocks away. He told them to stay behind the tree and he would be right by to pick them up. He pulled the car up by the tree and they ran out and got in the car and locked the doors. The guy saw them and came running towards the car and and motioned them to stop. Abel kept going and the guy started shaking his fist at them and was chasing the car down the road; fortunately, the traffic was clear and they made their getaway.

Back at the building, Silvia and Mary told the rest of us what had happened in the Church and how they sensed something was wrong, hiding behind the tree and the Church agent trying to stop them. Abel said he would be trading the car off the next day. We all wondered how they suspected Silvia and Mary. Did they think we were related to Bob somehow? Well, for sure, we better not go there, is what we all thought in unison. Abel said we may have to rely on the hardware man, Stewart, for a bit till we come up with another plan.

Gbezx called and introduced us to his assistant, Ibek, and said that he had to leave then and would be very busy for the next few days. Ibek would be working with us and then had a message for David. Ibek started with a, "Yes, David. We would like you to go to the big park about a mile from where you are. Go this evening just after dusk and be sure you take your night vision binoculars. Go out to the middle of the park and wait for the Four Horsemen, who will join you. They have a very important message from the Master. The Horseman called Famine, is the spokesman."

So, I went to the park, looking back occasionally. I waited for a few minutes and all four of them appeared and came up to me in formation. Famine said in his gravelly voice, "The Master wants you to go to Moscow and help out Boris, who asked for you. Your passport, other ID, rubies and clothing will be sent up to you in the elevator. Also, your round trip tickets to Frankfurt on Lufthansa Airlines. From there, you will go on a small twenty-passenger plane named Blu Skys to Moscow to meet Boris, who will meet you at the airport."

Back to the Streets of Moscow

A homeless man came up to us and started yelling. The Horseman War moved his steed forward and hit the man in the side of his head with the flat side of his spear, knocking the guy unconscious. He pulled his horse back in the formation. Famine said that was all for the message he had and they turned around in unison, took a few steps and then vanished. I went back and collected the items from the elevator, and Abel took me to the airport.

I arrived at Moscow airport with no hitches. In the Blu Sky seating area was Boris. I walked over to him, pulling my carry-on bag. I sat down one seat over from him, looking straight ahead.

Boris said hello and said the man seated behind us was his assistant Ivan. I looked quickly and then stared back ahead. I told them I had a stomach issue and must go to the toilet. Boris said to take my bag with me. A few minutes later, I came out of the restroom, and about fifty feet ahead of me was Boris with two big guys in gray overcoats that had their arms in his. Holy crap! I thought, they have arrested him. I looked over to where Ivan was; he had moved about three rows over and onto the end seat. I walked over by him and stared out the big windows.

He said, "Get out of here, fast."

I approached the Blu Sky kiosk and got in line behind about three people. As my eyes scanned the surroundings, a sense of unease washed over me. Emerging from the distance, making their way along the walkway, were three formidable figures clad in somber grey overcoats. Their stern countenances and presence sent a shiver down my spine.

I found myself standing behind a lady with a young child who couldn't have been more than three years old. An idea popped into my mind, and I motioned subtly to the woman, silently requesting permission to hold her little one. She nodded okay, and with confusion and nerves, I scooped the child into my arms. I did it, hoping the agents would think I was his father. The agents, none the wiser, continued on their way down past the other airline ticket booths, their attention drifting away from us as they pressed forward, oblivious to the ruse.

At about that time, we all started boarding the plane to Frankfurt, Germany. I was so nervous my heart was ready to jump out of my chest. We taxied out onto the runway and took off. I took some large breaths and could finally relax. I wondered what had happened to Boris and wondered if Ivan escaped. I was never able to find out and wondered what information the KGB would have already gotten out of them during torture. I was able to get to Quebec City Jean Lesage airport. I called Silvia and told her I needed a ride back. She said she would pick me up in about forty-five minutes, depending on traffic.

She picked me up in an old brown Ford station wagon. I asked her why I rated a pickup by the boss, and she said,

"Maybe I just wanted to see you."

Back home, I narrated my thrilling story to them all. They all said the same thing, "You got so lucky." Erik said, laughing, "Sometimes you are better to be lucky than good." I said, "I agree." My friends also had news. The hardware clerk, Stewart, informed them that his friend, the Church janitor, had discovered a freshly dug grave far behind the old

Church cemetery. He asked one of the Priests about it, and the Priest said not to worry about it and to forget he saw it. We all talked about poor Bob. Silvia told Abel to be cautious about meeting Stewart and maybe change their meeting place.

That evening, Maria, our cook, outdid herself with tender lamb chops, potato pancakes, sautéed asparagus in butter and garlic, and my favorite lemon meringue pie for dessert. That meal was a dream come alive. We then had a meeting, and Silvia was leading it. She started the discussion with, "We all need to get out in the city and pass out anti-Christion and political flyers. There is always some event going on." She pulled out a couple of recent local newspapers and read off some of the gatherings. There was one about Union members striking for higher wages, which was good for talking to people and giving out political pamphlets.

She said, "It starts at about 10 AM tomorrow at city hall. Alice and David, why don't you go to that one? Abel and Erick, a group of these people, are protesting a proposed Iow-cost housing project in their neighborhood. The paper calls them NlMBY's, which means Not In My Back Yard. When you hand them out, it is best to talk to the person to get their feelings, hand them a flyer, and say somebody like a person just gave me this paper. You might find some value in it." We finished off the evening with a glass of Cherrie.

Silvia was at the room's rear desk and motioned for me to come over. She asked in a low voice, "Care to join me in bed tonight?" And as much as I wanted to, I simply replied, "I'm sorry, but today's events shook me up. Can we wait till tomorrow night?" She said,

"Of course, I understand."

The next day, with Abel driving, Alice, Erik, and I piled into the old brown station wagon. Abel dropped off Alice and me at the hotel where the workers were striking. There were about a hundred people there, including some Teamster union members, as we discovered. One of the strikers gave Alice a sign that said, "Unfair to Workers," and told her to show it to the TV reporters with a van. Many people were raising their fists and shouting, so I did, too. More people were joining the crowd. Someone in the crowd would occasionally punch another person, calling them nasty communists or something.

Some commie party members were handing out flyers as we planned on doing. Soon, at least twenty individuals were punching and kicking each other. Some of the non-union members also joined the fray. One took a swing at me, but since I used to be a Navy SEAL, I was able to disable him quickly. Some woman jumped on my back, and I bent over quickly and shook her off. I looked for Alice in this mess and found her near the TV station van.

Her face was red; some woman had slapped her hard. Alice was frightened and wanted to leave right away. Some guy came rushing up cursing, and I hit him on the chin and knocked him out. I took Alices' arm and led her through the combatants. We walked about a block, and I stopped to console Alice, who was shaking and crying. I called Abel and told him we needed to get out of there fast. He said, "Only a few people showed up at the housing project, so I will be right over."

That evening, all of us watched TV to see if we had made the evening news, and sure enough, they caught a brief shot of Alice crying by the TV van. Her hands were in her face, so you couldn't really see who she was.

Alice was apologizing for being so out of control of her emotions. Mary came over and gave her a big hug, and consoled her. I said, "It was a tough situation, Alice. You didn't know who was who, and it was okay to react the way you did. I panicked too and got us out of the brawl as soon as possible, but again, it is okay." Silvia added, "We should report this to lbek." In about thirty minutes, he came online, and I explained the whole story. He asked if my picture had been taken, and I said, "I don't think so, as the TV cameraman was trying to fend off one of the participants. We didn't see me on the newscast."

"Were you real careful, Abel? Are you sure you weren't followed after you picked up David and Alice? He asked. "Yes, I drove around and doubled back a few times, and if we were, I'm sure we lost them," Abel said. He also said that he would trade in the car tomorrow.

Ibek said he would talk to Gbezx and the Master about what to do. He said to stay put as much as we could in the building. That evening, Maria made Honduras specialties for us, which was very good but a touch spicy. We had a long chat about our poor luck lately over a couple of bottles of good wine that Erik provided. Mary mentioned that we should find out where the Socialists and Marxists met. Many didn't believe in God, and could be a source of information and could even become members for us. It sounded like a good idea, is what Silvia said. Erik said he would go online and find out what he could. Abel said maybe he should sneak out and go to the hardware store to see what the clerk, Stewart, had found out from his janitor contact at the Church. He said he needed to change cars anyway.

The next day, Abel changed cars with the shady dealer and drove carefully over to the hardware store. He parked in the back, walked around the store twice, and then went inside. Stewart was busy with a customer, so he went over and was looking at a new lawn mower when another clerk came over and asked him if he had any questions. Able said no, "Just looking." The clerk said, "Oh, you are Stewart's friend, aren't you?" Abel was shocked but managed to mumble no and that Stewart had helped him with some repair issues. The clerk said goodbye and went to help another customer. Abel wondered if he was busted, if Stewart was a double agent, or if the other clerk was an agent, etc. Just about then, Stewart came over. Abel told him what happened. Stewart said he was kind of a busybody, and it was harmless. Stewart had been helping someone else with some home repairs, and that's why he told him to approach Abel. You had better buy something, is what Stewart said. Good idea, Abel said, and bought a screwdriver and a couple of light bulbs we needed. Stewart said there was going to be another big meeting at the Church next week and that he could find out where if we wanted. I said okay; I gave Stewart 50 Canadian dollars, paid for my stuff, and left.

Back at the property, Abel told the rest what had happened and asked if we wanted to try to listen to the upcoming secret meeting. Mary said David could go and wear a Priests gown and hide up where he did before and if they asked him what he was doing, he could say he was meditating. Silvia said we better find out what it was about before we all went into trouble. I asked Abel if he felt confident that the other clerk at the hardware store was right. "Well, I can't be absolutely sure, but I think he is just a friendly guy trying to make people happy," Abel replied. We just then got a call from Gbezx; he asked that I go down to the Underworld to meet with him ASAP. I put on lighter clothes, got in the elevator and went down. Gbezx and Ibek met me and we went to Gbezx's office. Ibek appeared around the same as Gbezx but was maybe six inches shorter and had a rather high-pitched voice.

Gbezx said, "David, I'm going to close the office where you are at. We will assign Silvia and Mary to our operation office in Paris, France. Silvia will replace the controller who is there and is quite ill. Mary will remain as her assistant. There are big conflicts erupting there between the Muslim refugee population and the native French people. This is good for us as it ferments distrust and hatred between them. Also, the political parties are at loggerheads with the Liberals and Conservatives butting heads over social issues, not unlike many countries in the world. Erik and Alice were to go to Toronto, Canada, where we have a computer center that we are expanding. We don't feel Alice has the temperament to be in the field. She is good on the computer and Erik can help her get better. Abel wanted to go to Edmonton, Canada, as a lady friend of his is there that we transferred about six months ago. We are going to make a deal with Maria, who has relatives who live in the area and need inexpensive housing, to allow all of them to live there at no cost. We will also pay all of their costs and expenses. We will close off the elevator. There will be a phone line where she can reach us in an emergency. So that leaves you, David. We are promoting you to a mobile troubleshooter agent, reporting only to Ibek, me and the Master. We will send you around to French, Spanish and English-speaking countries. You will have a room in Paris where Silvia will be located for a home base. How does that sound to you, he asked."

"Sounds exciting," I said.

"Okay, you need to go back and help the others pack. Mary and Silvia will arrange transportation for everyone. You are to send some of the sensitive material down here to be archived or destroyed. Tell Abel to take the car and park it on the street with the keys in it and the driver's window down."

Gbezx also said he would call and talk to each one of my office mates to give them instructions now.

"David, come with me," Ibek said.

"Do you feel like having a good walk?"

"I'm with you," I said.

"We are going to see The Master. He likes to hear your stories."

On our way, we went by the Treasury. Ibek asked if I had seen it and I said no. "Well, let's let you have a peek," and with that, he knocked on a tall bronze door. A devil opened it and seeing it was Ibek motioned us in. It was overwhelming; the room was at least the size of an American football field and about thirty feet high. There were long tables with an aisle in the center that was covered with bundles of currency from all of the countries of the world about three feet high. It must be hundreds of billions, I thought.

As we continued towards the back, in between the tables, there were twenty heavy steel tables, maybe thirty feet long and three feet wide. They were loaded with large gold ingots stacked two feet tall, literally tons of gold. Then, ten more tables with bins full of thousands of silver and gold coins.

As we continued back about 100 yards to the end of the room, there were tables with trays of uncut diamonds and other precious stones. The walls were covered with thousands of antique weapons, daggers, swords, lances, spears, all types of old flintlock rifles, and pistols. When I was on a trip to Moscow, they had an Armory there as well, but it didn't compare to this collection. There were shields like the Knights Templar bore when I saw them in the Church, and all types of modern arms as well. This was so unbelievable; my heart was pounding and I was getting a bit lightheaded. I asked Ibek what he thought of all this. He said it doesn't relate to him as it does to me. We walked down the aisle to the entrance and I turned around for another look to take it all in again and I thought I could see why it was nothing to him, just metal and rocks!

We walked for about another mile and came to Lucifer's office and were ushered in. Lucifer was at his desk typing something on his computer. He motioned us to sit down. He said he was short-selling 100,000 shares of Tesla stock just for the fun of it. My God, I thought, Master playing the stock market? How could this be? I was not sure if he was kidding or not. He finished his transaction and then turned to us.

"So, David, Gbezx told me he is closing the operation you were part of. This is a wise decision. As you say, it is better to be safe than sorry. Are you happy with your assignment?"

"Yes and thank you for asking," I said.

I asked him what ever happened to the Russian, Boris. Ibek said he would like to answer it for me. "Go ahead," Lucifer said. Ibek said one of their good contacts over there told him that as soon as his arms were free, Boris injected himself with the poison ring he was wearing and died within half an hour. The Major, who was in charge, was really pissed off at the two arresting officers for letting him have his arms free. Now, they couldn't interrogate him.

"Wow, I'm so sorry to hear that," I said, "And what happened to Ivan?"

"After you went to the airline booth, he was able to slip out through a service door onto the tarmac and made his way back to his quarters and warn the others because he didn't know about Boris's situation. We are working on the problem now."

"I'm sorry to hear about Boris, but happy Ivan was able to escape," is all that I could say.

Lucifer said Boris was a good agent and served us well and said I hear you had a visit from my Horseman recently; they told me what happened. Yes, I did. They are a scary gang and I didn't know how they appeared and disappeared as quickly. That is my secret, he said. He pulled back his head and laughed his melodious, loud laugh.

"Anything else you want to say?" He asked. I shook my head no.

"Ibek, can you please take David back to the elevator so he can go back up and help his companions get ready to move." Ibek and I walked to the elevator and I went up. Everyone was talking at once about the re-assignments and all the things we needed to move and send down below, etc. I walked into the kitchen and asked Maria what she thought about her situation. There were tears in her eyes, and she said this would be wonderful as her daughter and her three children and her husband, who had got laid off recently, and her sister and one child, who was going to college, would have a good place to live without any costs. She said the Master is very generous. She said she was making a big Caesar salad with lots of shrimp for dinner. I said I was looking forward to it.

Back in the meeting room, Silvia and Mary were drawing up some priorities on a big whiteboard, and the others were making suggestions. I kept quiet—the old saying, "Sometimes it is better to remain quiet and thought a fool than to open your mouth and remove all doubt," came to me. I didn't have much to do other than pack my bag and join Silvia and Mary on a flight to our new home base in Paris.

That evening at Maria's Caesar salad dinner, there were, of course, a lot of conversations about how we would all miss each other, etc. Gbezx had told Silvia it was not a panic situation about the move time but to try to move it along in a reasonable manner. Erik said there would be quite a lot of electronics and communication issues to handle. Alice said she would help him out. Abel said he would be available to help in any capacity that was needed.

Amidst the enticing promises of help and unwavering support, there was an unspoken question hanging in the air. It felt heavy, like the scent of rain before a storm. This question was about our ultimate destinies, the mysterious force that guided our lives. Could our determination and hard work really shape our futures, or were we just passengers on the unpredictable sea of fate, heading into the unknown? As the night went on, this haunting question lingered in our minds, a puzzle we could only hope to solve in the next part of our journey.

Epilogue Teaser

As you've reached the final page of this journey, you may have noticed that not all mysteries have been unraveled. Some questions remain unanswered, and deeper truths lie just beneath the surface, waiting to be revealed.

But fear not—the story is far from over. The next chapter promises to be even more intense, filled with twists, revelations, and the answers you've been seeking. In **Book 2**, the unsolved mysteries from this first installment will come to light, pulling you further into the intrigue and excitement.

Stay tuned, as the sequel is on its way. **Book 2** will be coming soon !